ROMANIAN GYMNASTICS

The Romanian Gymnastics Federation
1906–1996

Cover Photo: Alexandra Marinescu by Eileen Langsley
Back Cover: (center, top) Daniela Silivaş
(left to right, bottom) Nadia Comăneci, Cristina Bontaş, Lavinia Miloşovici, Ecaterina Szabo, Aurelia Dobre.
All Photos Courtesy of the Romanian Gymnastics Federation

ROMANIAN GYMNASTICS

Kurt W. Treptow

With a Foreword by
Nicolae Vieru
President of the Romanian Gymnastics Federation

The Center for Romanian Studies
Las Vegas ◊ Oxford ◊ Palm Beach

Published in the United States of America by
Histria Books, a division of Histria LLC
7181 N. Hualapai Way
Las Vegas, NV 89166 USA
HistriaBooks.com

The Center for Romanian Studies is an imprint of Histria Books. Titles published under the imprints of Histria Books are distributed worldwide exclusively by the Casemate Group.

Front cover photo: Alexandra Marinescu by Eileen Langsley

Library of Congress Control Number: 2019952973

ISBN 978-9-73577-031-0 (case bound)
ISBN 978-1-59211-048-3 (softbound)
ISBN 978-1-59211-049-0 (e-book)

CONTENTS

PREFACE

Since Nadia Comăneci stunned the world with her amazing success at the 1976 Olympic Games in Montreal, Romania has become identified internationally with the sport of gymnastics. As the twentieth anniversary of Nadia's receiving the first perfect ten awarded in Olympic history approached in 1996, the Romanian Gymnastics program looked back upon twenty years of sustained success. With this in mind, the publication of a book dedicated to Romanian Gymnastics was long overdue to commemorate a program that had produced many great gymnasts and numerous international titles, including the two-time Romanian Women's Gymnastics Team that would represent the country at the Olympic Games in Atlanta in 1996 and that would go on ultimately to win five consecutive World Championship titles: Brisbane in 1994, Sabae in 1995, Lausanne in 1997, Tianjin in 1999, and Ghent in 2001.

On the occasion of the centennial of the modern Olympic Games, the Center for Romanian Studies, in cooperation with the Romanian Gymnastics Federation, prepared this volume on the history of Romanian gymnastics. The volume also commemorated the ninetieth anniversary of the founding of the Romanian Gymnastics Federation in 1906. This full color album includes a brief presentation of the history and culture of Romania for those wishing to learn more about this fascinating country, as well as a presentation of each of the members of the 1996 Romanian Women's Gymnastics team, including such great gymnasts as Lavinia Miloşovici, Gina Gogean, and Simona Amânar.

This second printing is issued on the occasion of the 2020 Olympic Games in Tokyo, Japan, where, unfortunately, Romania will not be participating in the team competition. Nonetheless, the remarkable contribution that this small country has made to the sport of gymnastics shall never be forgotten and is commemorated in this album.

I want to acknowledge the generous assistance of the many people who made this volume possible: Alexandru Mironov, Minister of Youth and Sport, Nicolae Vieru, President of the Romanian Gymnastics Federation, Cristian Țopescu of the Romanian National Television, and Octavian Belu, coach of the National Women's Team, for their generous support of this project, as well as the members of the 1996 National Women's Gymnastics Team for their cooperation in realizing the material contained in this book. I also want to thank Aurel Vîrlan of Rompres and Vasile Buţă of the Romanian Television for their work on the photographs and video footage used in preparing this volume. The photographic and video material used in this project was provided courtesy of the Romanian Gymnastics Federation, Rompres, and the Romanian National Television to whom we express our gratitude.

Dr. Kurt W. Treptow

Nadia Comăneci

FOREWORD BY NICOLAE VIERU
PRESIDENT OF THE ROMANIAN GYMNASTICS FEDERATION

The Romanian Gymnastics Federation was founded in 1906 and is one of the oldest sports federations in Romania, as well as throughout the world. In 1907 it became the ninth national federation to join the International Gymnastics Federation.

As it celebrates its 90th anniversary, the Romanian Gymnastics Federation is proud to cooperate in the publication of this work — initiated and carried out by Professor Kurt W. Treptow of the Center for Romanian Studies in Iaşi — a work that includes a short history of gymnastics in Romania, the recording of our international results, as well as a presentation of the 1996 Romanian Women's Gymnastics team for the Olympic Games in Atlanta, an event that will mark twenty years of glorious success for Romania.

As for tradition, mention should be made of the bronze medals obtained at the 1956 Olympic Games in Melbourne, the 1958 Moscow World Championships, and the 1960 Rome Olympic Games in the team competition, as well as the silver and bronze medals obtained in the European Championship in Bucharest in 1957 and Cracow in 1959.

A record of the results of Romanian gymnastics between 1975 and 1995 demonstrates that this has been a period of remarkable success:

	Olympic Games	World Championships	European Championships (Seniors)	TOTAL
Gold Medals	15	27	44	86
Silver Medals	14	23	29	65
Bronze Medals	13	22	27	61
TOTAL	42	72	101	214

Throughout these years, our Federation has produced many great personalities of the sport, athletes whose performances often verged on the artistic, such as Nadia Comăneci, Dan Grecu, Ecaterina Szabo, Daniela Silivaş, Aurelia Dobre, Simona Păuca, Cristina Bontaş, Lavinia Miloşovici, Gina Gogean, and Marius Urzică, as well as renowned coaches such as Bela Karolyi, Adrian Goreac, Octavian Belu, and Dan Grecu, among others.

We are proud that our federation, through the activities of its athletes, coaches, and its representatives in the International Federation, has substantially contributed to the overall development and high standards of world gymnastics. Romanian coaches are continuously asked to work abroad, and the already considerable number that do so contribute to the increasingly high level of world gymnastics.

The remarkable results achieved thus far have brought to Romanian gymnastics a well–deserved prestige, consistently ranking near the top in the world hierarchy. All these achievements are primarily the result of the talent and tenacious efforts of our athletes and their coaches, the system of training and selection, a system whose premise is based on a permanent and rigorous contact with local clubs, and also skillful timing, commensurate with the possibilities of the age of the athletes.

Gymnastics is highly regarded and extremely popular in Romania. Many top women and men gymnasts have often received the title of "best athletes of the year." After the December 1989 Revolution gymnastics has been supported by the Ministry of Youth and Sports and the Romanian Olympic Committee. Today, the federation enjoys independence and autonomy, no longer censored by the dictatorship, which in the past inhibited international exchanges. In the years since the Revolution, the specific activity of the federation expanded tremendously, particularly on the foreign relations level, a freedom enjoyed both by clubs throughout the country.

The information contained in this short study and the excellent results of the Romanian gymnastics program and its continuity over the past two decades, all illustrate the strength of Romanian gymnastics and the international prestige it enjoys, and, at the same time, reveal the premises for its future success.

Finally, I would like to thank Professor Kurt W. Treptow for his outstanding effort in realizing the publication of this book.

ROMANIA
A LAND OF TRADITION AND WONDER

Located in East Central Europe, Romania is a beautiful land, rich in diversity and culture. It is crossed in the center by the Carpathian Mountains which provide breathtakingly beautiful scenery and include some of Romania's most remarkable tourist attractions, including the Peleş Castle in Sinaia and the world-renowned painted monasteries of northern Moldavia. To the south, the country is bordered by the Danube River. Near the Iron Gates, at Drobeta-Turnu Severin, the ruins of the bridge built by the Roman Emperor Trajan can still be seen. The vast plains in the southern part of the country, known as Wallachia, have great agricultural potential. In this region, the capital city of Bucharest is located. Today a modern metropolis of over two million inhabitants, Bucharest, with its many architectural treasures, was once known as the Paris of the East. The Black Sea coast and the Danube Delta with its scenic beauty, fascinating wildlife, and favorable summer climate are favorite vacation spots for tourists from throughout the world. The eastern part of the country, known as Moldavia, is rich in tradition and full of beauty. The landscape is dotted with historical monuments, among them monasteries from the fifteenth and sixteenth centuries, such as Voroneţ and Suceviţa, famous for their exterior mural paintings. One of the most beautiful cities in the country, Iaşi, built on seven hills and filled with historical and religious treasures, is the traditional capital of this region, and is often referred to as the cultural capital of Romania.

The Monastery of Suceviţa
The sixteenth century church is world renowned for its exterior mural paintings.

Finally, the western part of the country, Transylvania, is a land steeped in Romanian tradition. The cradle of Romanian civilization and the heart of the former Roman province of Dacia, it was here that the Romanian people were formed. A region of cultural interaction throughout the centuries, the atmosphere in Transylvania is further enriched by the cultural contributions of the Hungarian and German minority populations. Cities such as Sibiu and

11

Sighişoara are museums in and of themselves. With its forests, plains, mountains, hills, sea coast, and favorable continental climate, Romania is a land of cultural and geographic diversity, a land of tradition and wonder, that offers something for everyone.

Throughout their long history, the Romanian lands have always been an area of diversity and interaction. For centuries they have been a borderland between Orthodoxy and Catholicism, between Christianity and Islam, and between the various empires that have exerted their domination over this region of Europe. This has contributed to the complexity of Romanian history, just as it inhibited development and delayed the formation of a Romanian national state until the middle of the nineteenth century. Soviet domination after World War II further halted development. Potentially the wealthiest and most important state in Southeastern Europe, it is only since the overthrow of the communist regime in December 1989 that the Romanian nation again has the opportunity to affirm itself freely as a member of the European community.

Romania is bordered by Bulgaria to the south, Yugoslavia and Hungary to the west, the Ukraine to the north and east, and the Romanian territory of Bessarabia, today known as the Republic of Moldavia (Moldova), to the east. The country is crossed by the Carpathian Mountains and the Danube River, and borders on the Black Sea.

The Romanian lands have been inhabited since ancient times. During antiquity, an Indo-European population, the Geto-Dacians, a Thracian tribe, inhabited the present-day territory of Romania, which was then known as Dacia. In addition, several Greek colonies were established along the Black Sea Coast. The first to mention the Geto-Dacians was the Greek historian Herodotus who referred to them as "the most manly and law abiding of the Thracian tribes." During the first century B.C. a powerful Geto-Dacian kingdom was founded by Burebista (70-44 B.C.), encompassing most of present-day Romania. This kingdom became a powerful threat to the expanding Roman Empire. Just before his assassination, Julius Ceasar was preparing an expedition against the Geto-Dacians, but the death of Burebista that same year ended the danger as the kingdom became fragmented. Rome extended its influence south of the Danube, only to be challenged by the Geto-Dacian King Decebal (A.D. 87-106), who reestablished a powerful kingdom north of the Danube. This led the Roman Emperor Trajan to lead expeditions in A.D. 105-106 that resulted in the conquest of Dacia and its transformation into a Roman province.

The Monument Tropaeum Traiani at Adamclisi
**Built by the Roman Emperor Trajan
to commemorate his victories over the Dacians**

Over the next 165 years, Roman colonization led to the adoption of Latin as the language of communication and the adoption of many Roman customs. This process led to the formation of a Dacian-Romanian people by the time Roman administration was withdrawn from the province in A.D. 271. Bound together by Christianity which began to penetrate into the region already in the second century, this population would evolve over the next several centuries to form the Romanian people. This people resisted the waves of barbarian invaders that swarmed into Europe after the fall of the Roman Empire and preserved its unique identity, at times assimilating the less numerous invading peoples.

As the barbarian invasions of the early Middle Ages began to subside, by the tenth century historical sources mention the appearance of several small Romanian state formations on the territory of present-day Romania. The unification of these small state structures led to the creation of the first independent Romanian principality, Wallachia, at the end of the thirteenth century. By the middle of the next century, a second independent Romanian principality, Moldavia, was established along the eastern slopes of the Carpathians.

The third Romanian land, Transylvania, fell under the control of the Hungarian kingdom beginning in the eleventh century, but maintained its individual identity as a separate principality. The Romanians, who formed the vast majority of the population in that region, were denied political rights and ruled over by an alliance of Hungarian noblemen, Szecklers, and Saxon colonists.

From their foundation, Wallachia and Moldavia played an important role in European history, protecting the trade routes that crossed their territory, linking Central Europe and the Black Sea. Although the Romanians lived in three separate principalities during the

Vlad III Dracula
Prince of Wallachia
(1448, 1456-1462, 1476)

Middle Ages, economic, political, and cultural ties between them were never interrupted. With the expansion of the powerful Ottoman Empire into Europe, the three principalities faced a difficult period as they struggled to maintain their autonomy. Their resistance to Ottoman expansion drew attention throughout Europe. The deeds of many of Romanian leaders became subjects of European folklore. The best-known example is Prince Vlad III Dracula of Wallachia who became identified with the fictional vampire created by Bram Stoker. The true Dracula was a capable prince who sought to preserve the autonomy of his principality. Meanwhile, his cousin, Prince Stephen the Great of Moldavia, during his brilliant reign of forty-seven years, fought the

Turks and preserved the autonomy of his land. His deeds were praised throughout Europe and the Pope in Rome proclaimed him an "Athlete of Christ." He also built many remarkable religious and historical monuments that can still be visited today. Likewise, the Romanian-born governor of Hungary, John Hunyadi, defended Transylvania from the Ottoman threat, gaining renown in the capitals of Europe. His family castle in Hunedoara remains as a monument to this leader who defended both Europe and the Romanian lands from the Turkish threat and is a popular tourist destination. Although they gradually came under Ottoman domination during the fifteenth and sixteenth centuries, through the struggles led by these leaders the principalities managed to preserve their identity, paying tribute to the Sultan instead of being incorporated within the Ottoman Empire.

Hunedoara Castle

An important event in Romanian history occurred in 1600 with the momentary union of the three Romanian principalities, Wallachia, Moldavia, and Transylvania, under the rule of Prince Michael the Brave (1593-1601). Although his achievement was short-lived (he was assassinated in 1601), his deed remained as a symbol of the Romanians' struggle for national unity.

At the end of the seventeenth and the beginning of the eighteenth centuries important changes took place in the political situation of the Romanian countries. Following the expansion of Austria toward the southeast that began after the Turks failed at the siege of Vienna in 1683, Transylvania became a principality within the Hapsburg Empire. After Russia approached the boundaries of Moldavia during the reign of Peter the Great, and the Hapsburg Empire occupied Transylvania, the Ottoman Empire changed its system of governing the Romanian lands to prevent the emancipation of the two Danubian principalities, introducing the Phanariot regime in Moldavia and Wallachia at the beginning of the eighteenth century. During this period, the Ottomans appointed princes loyal to the empire from among the Greek aristocracy in Istanbul, most of whom lived in a district known as the Phanar. The governors of the Principality of Transylvania were now named directly by the Court of Vienna. During the century of Phanariot rule (1711/1716-1821), despite the oppressive form of the Ottoman domination in terms of rigorous political control and economic exploitation, important fiscal, social, administrative, and judicial reforms were realized, including the abolition of serfdom. Throughout this period the two countries managed to maintain their autonomy despite increasing interference in their internal affairs by the Ottoman Porte. Following the Treaty of Bucharest in 1812, ending the Russo-Turkish War, the eastern

Michael the Brave
The first prince to unite the Romanian lands
under one ruler.

part of Moldavia, known as Bessarabia, was occupied by Tsarist Russia.

Throughout this difficult period, a sense of ethnic and later national consciousness began to develop among Romanian intellectuals. Education in the Romanian language began and the bases for the development of modern Romanian literature were laid. Further developments and socioeconomic conflicts led to the outbreak of revolutions in all three Romanian lands in 1848-1849. The revolutions had as their principal objectives national liberty, improvement of the condition of the peasantry, the equality of rights of all citizens, and the elimination of foreign interference in the internal affairs of the Romanian lands. Although they were defeated, the Revolutions of 1848-1849 marked the beginning of a movement for unification among the Romanians of all three lands that would grow and develop during the following decades. Following 1848 political, social, and cultural life in Wallachia and Moldavia were dominated by the idea of unification of the two principalities.

The realization of the union of the principalities was made possible by the defeat of Russia during the Crimean War (1853-1856). In the summer of 1857 assemblies in Iaşi and Bucharest, with delegates representing all social classes participating, unanimously voted in favor of the unification of the two principalities in a single state with the name Romania. Despite objections by the Great Powers, Romanians in Moldavia (on 5 January 1859) and Wallachia (on 24 January 1859) both elected Alexandru Ioan Cuza as their prince, bringing about, through their own initiative, the *de facto* unification of the principalities. Prince Alexandra Ioan Cuza and his principal collaborator, Mihail Kogălniceanu, initiated a series of important reforms that laid the basis for the modern Romanian state. The abdication of Alexandra Ioan Cuza on 11 February 1866, as a result of a plot by opponents, led to the installation of a foreign prince, Carol I, of the German Hohenzollern-Sigmaringen family.

The reign of Carol I (prince from 1866-1881 and king of Romania from 1881-1914) introduced the period of constitutional monarchy in Romania. A new constitution, with a liberal character, created the conditions for the formation of a pluralist political system based on the alternation of governance between two political parties, the Conservatives and the National Liberals, with an unequal electoral system. The new regime assured the fundamental liberties of citizens and made possible the progressive integration of the country in Western European values. The economy of the country developed, led by commerce and industry. The Liberal governments laid the bases for modern capitalist economic and financial institutions. Freedom of opinion and the rapid development of the country had its impact on culture as well, which produced some of its most representative personalities. The

Mihai Eminescu

most important of these was the national poet Mihai Eminescu (1850-1889), who was also a remarkable journalist. Romania proclaimed its independence from the Ottoman Empire on 9 May 1877, and participated alongside Russia in the war against the Turks.

In 1881 Romania became a kingdom, an event that marked the sovereignty and independence of the country both domestically and internationally. The continual threat posed by Russia determined the leadership of the country to enter into an alliance with the Central Powers in 1883. With the achievement of national independence, Romanians in neighboring territories still under foreign domination began to look to Bucharest for inspiration. In Transylvania (which had been included in Hungary as a result of the creation of the Dual Monarchy in 1867) the Romanian National Party played an important role in the intensification of the struggle for national liberation of the Romanians in this province.

The last stage in the process of the creation of the modern unified national state took place amidst the final phases of World War I and the social and national agitation that accompanied the collapse of the multinational empires of Austria-Hungary and Tsarist Russia. The principal political leader of Romania during this time and the architect of the creation of the unified national state was Prime Minister Ion I.C. Brătianu. On 9 April 1918 Bessarabia united with Romania. Later the same year, as a result of the collapse of the Central Powers, the Romanians of Bucovina (28 November 1918) and Transylvania (1 December 1918) also voted to unite with the Kingdom of Romania, thus completing the process of national unification begun in 1859. Thanks in part to the skillful diplomacy of Ion I.C. Brătianu, this reality was recognized by a series of international treaties in the years immediately following the war. On 28 June 1919 Romania became a founding member of the League of Nations.

The Table of Silence
Part of the sculptural complex created by the Romanian-born sculptor Constantin Brâncuşi in Târgu Jiu to commemorate those who died in World War I

The creation of Greater Romania was followed by a series of structural reforms: the adoption of a new electoral system that allowed for universal suffrage (1918), an agrarian reform (1921) that liquidated the great estates giving the land to the peasants, and the adoption of a new constitution (1923). These measures enlarged the democratic basis of the pluralist political system.

In foreign affairs Romania initiated a series of political and diplomatic actions designed to consolidate the unified national state, to maintain its national sovereignty, and to protect its territorial integrity, by working to preserve the status quo in Europe. Together with Czechoslovakia and Yugoslavia, Romania laid the basis for the Little Entente (1920-1921) and concluded, together with Turkey and Greece, the Balkan Entente in 1934.

A sixteenth century Romanian icon depicting Christ being taken down from the cross.

The change in the balance of power in Central Europe with the rise of Nazi Germany forced Romania to draw closer to the Reich to counterbalance the threat posed by Soviet Russia. At the outbreak of World War II Romania proclaimed its neutrality (4 September 1939). After the surrender of France and the defeat of Great Britain on the continent, the situation of Romania worsened. Following an ultimatum from the Soviet Union on 26 June 1940, in accordance with the terms of the Molotov-Ribbentrop Pact signed in August 1939, the USSR forcibly occupied Bessarabia and the northern part of Bucovina (a territory not mentioned in the Hitler-Stalin Pact and that had never been part of Russia or the Ukraine). Two months later, Germany and Italy imposed the Diktat of Vienna (30 August 1940) on Romania which was forced to cede northern Transylvania, where Romanians comprised the majority of the population, to Hungary. In addition, Romania agreed to return the Quadrilateral (part of southern Dobrodgea that had been acquired in the Second Balkan War in 1913) to Bulgaria through the Treaty of Craiova on 7 September 1940. Following these disasters and compromises, the king, Carol II, was compelled to abdicate (6 September 1940) in favor of his son Michael I (1940-1947). Leadership of the state was assumed by General Ion Antonescu together with the Legionary Movement. After months of feuding, a power struggle between the general and the Legionaries erupted into a brief civil war in January 1941 that resulted in Antonescu consolidating his control over the state with the help of the German army. Thus, a military dictatorship replaced the National Legionary State that had been proclaimed on 14 September 1940.

On 22 June 1941 Romania entered the war on the side of Nazi Germany against the Soviet Union, both to regain the territories occupied by the Soviets in 1940 and because of continual Soviet provocations that further threatened the country. After initial successes, defeats on the Eastern front began to destroy Romanian morale. Amidst disputes over the proper course of action to take to withdraw from the war, King Michael I ordered the arrest of Ion Antonescu and his principal collaborators on 23 August 1944 and declared war on Nazi Germany. On 12 September 1944 an armistice was signed in Moscow between Romania and the Allied Powers, represented by the Soviet Union. Harsh terms were imposed by the victors, but the annulment of the Vienna Diktat was promised. As a result the Romanian army participated alongside the Red Army with an effective total of 540,000 troops to free Transylvania (25 October 1944) and to defeat Nazi Germany.

The result of the king's decision to conclude an immediate armistice, while hastening the end of the war, also allowed for continual Soviet interference in the internal affairs of the country. At Soviet insistence, on 6 March 1945, a communist government (under the guise of a multi-party coalition) under the leadership of Petru Groza was installed in Bucharest. The Soviet occupiers pillaged the country's industry and agriculture, together with their Romanian communist collaborators (who until 23 August 1944 had numbered only a few hundred), and began to purge all political opposition. Thousands died in communist prisons as a result. Finally, on 30 December 1947 King Michael was forced by the communist authorities to abdicate and the monarchy was abolished.

Under the communist regime all industry and banks were nationalized on 11 June 1948, and, after an intermediate stage of agrarian reform during the period when the Communists sought to consolidate their rule, agriculture was forcibly collectivized. The prewar elite of Romanian society either fled into exile or died in communist prisons. A strong resistance continued in the mountains and was only completely defeated by the communist regime in 1956. During the period of Stalinization, Romanian history was rewritten to suit Marxist ideology, the orthography of the language was changed so as to make it appear more Slavic, and Romanian culture was generally suppressed with many of its most representative works in all fields being forbidden by the pro-Soviet regime.

The Khrushchev regime's policy of de-Stalinization threatened the leadership of the Romanian Communist Party which began to change its policies so as to adopt a more nationalistic line, while never abandoning the principles of Marxism-Leninism. Party leader Gheorghe Gheorghiu-Dej, Secretary-General of the Communist Party, strengthened this policy after the departure of Soviet troops from Romania in 1958. Gheorghiu-Dej's successor, Nicolae Ceauşescu (1965-1989), continued the nationalist policies of his predecessor and allowed some economic and cultural liberalization during the early years of his rule. In August 1968 Romania publicly condemned the Warsaw Pact invasion of Czechoslovakia in which it had refused to participate. Ceauşescu was seen as a communist maverick in the west, refusing to follow the Soviet line on numerous occasions. Meanwhile, at home, after 1971, he began to exert ever greater control internally, creating a harsh Stalinist system intolerant of any opposition and stifling economic initiative. The state began to impose itself more strongly into every aspect of Romanian life. During the 1980s Ceauşescu initiated a draconian program to repay Romania's massive foreign debt causing the standard of living to fall dramatically as even the most basic goods were rationed.

Nadia Comăneci

A bright moment during this period of darkness was Romania's success in international sports competitions. Athletes such as Ilie Năstase, Ion Țiriac, Ivan Pațaichin, and others excelled in their respective sports. Romania achieved its greatest success in gymnastics beginning with Nadia Comăneci who awed the world at the 1976 Olympic Games in Montreal where she won three gold medals and was awarded seven perfect scores of ten for her performances.

After many years of hardship, deprived of freedom and facing shortages of even basic resources, in December 1989, amidst the collapse of communist regimes throughout Eastern Europe, a mass uprising of the Romanian people led to the overthrow of Nicolae Ceaușescu who, together with his wife Elena, was summarily tried and executed on 25 December. The overthrow of the Ceaușescu regime created the possibility for the reinstallation of a democratic system in Romania and its integration into European political and economic structures.

After the collapse of the communist regime in December 1989, a multi-party political system was reintroduced in Romania. Historical parties such as the National-Peasant Party and the National-Liberal Party were reestablished, and a variety of new parties including the Social Democracy Party of Romania, the Democratic Party-National Salvation Front, the Romanian National Unity Party, the Civic Alliance Party, and others were created. In addition a number of ethnic parties representing ethnic minorities in the country were formed, such as the Democratic Union of Hungarians in Romania. In addition, to the creation of a pluralist political system that ensures the rights of all nationalities, a market economy

The Seal of Romania

was introduced into Romania beginning in 1990 and the process of privatization of state-owned industries is well under way. In addition, the country has begun to take part in numerous European and international economic and security organizations, being one of the first former Soviet-bloc countries to adhere to the NATO alliance's "Partnership for Peace" program in 1994. In addition, Romanian culture has begun to flourish thanks to the new atmosphere of freedom within the country. At the same time, the Romanian tradition of excellence in sports has continued. The Romanian soccer team performed admirably at the 1994 World Championships in the United States, while the Romanian Women's Gymnastics Team has continued its history of success, winning the last two world championships.

Today, Romania is a democratic society, respecting the rights of all its citizens, regardless of ethnic or religious background, with a developing free market economy. Romania is a country of natural beauty, steeped in historic tradition, with great economic potential.

Bran Castle, near Braşov

One of the many unique historic monuments in Romania that attract visitors from all over the world.

A friendly, hospitable people, Romanians welcome visitors to their country.

Further Reading: *A History of Romania.* Ed. Kurt W. Treptow (Iaşi: Center for Romanian Studies, 1996).

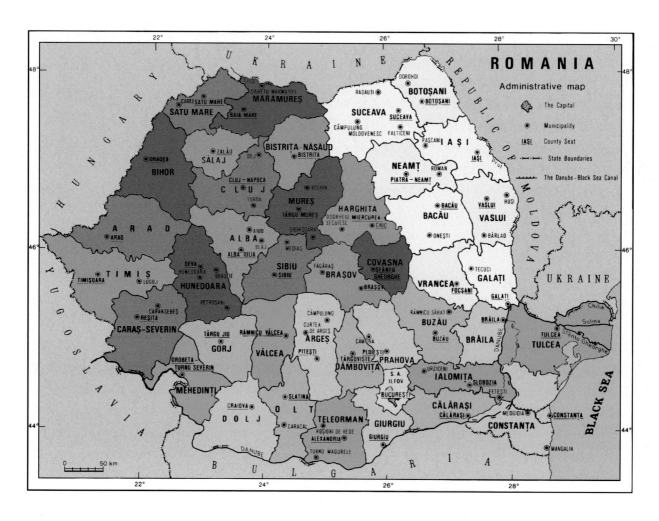

A SHORT HISTORY OF ROMANIAN GYMNASTICS

Documents reveal that during the seventeenth and eighteenth centuries, sundry celebrations and important events at the princely courts in the Romanian lands were accompanied by special athletic performances, such as acrobatic feats, tightrope balancing, jumping over as many as eight lined buffaloes, including one or even two somersaults, all these performed by local athletes *(pehlivani)* or renowned acrobats brought from abroad especially for this purpose.

In 1822, at Mediaş, a gymnastics association called *Turnverein* was founded. The Saxon school teacher Stephen Ludwig Roth included the German Friedrich Ludwig Jahn's gymnastics program in the school curriculum. A controversial figure, Jahn was the father of apparatus gymnastics.

Steven Ludwig Roth

Beginning in the 1860s, Romanian gymnastics programs further expanded through the founding of gymnastics associations and societies, such as those in Arad and Bistriţa in 1869, and Braşov in 1861. The society of weaponry, gymnastics, and target-shooting was founded in Bucharest in 1866, later to be called the "Skeet-Shooting Range." An international target-shooting and gymnastics society was also founded in Iaşi in 1877. Gymnastics societies were later founded in Timişoara and Craiova in 1889 and 1890 respectively. Others sprung up between 1891 and 1906 at Piteşti, Agnita, Târgu Jiu, Ploieşti, Galaţi, and Câmpulung-Muscel.

On 14 September 1906 a Congress of Gymnastics Societies took place, which founded the Romanian Gymnastics Federation, the first central institution to coordinate and lead the over eighteen societies existent throughout the country at that time. The first chairman was General P.V. Năsturel, with two deputies: then Minister of Education Spiru Haret and Lt. Colonel Theodor Petrescu. New gymnastics societies and clubs appeared in 1907, and that same year the Romanian Gymnastics Federation became the ninth national federation to join the International Gymnastics Federation. In May of the same year the first national gymnastics performances were given to the public at the Arenele Romane in Bucharest, with demonstrative acrobatics on the high bar, uneven parallel bars, and pommel horse.

Gheorghe Moceanu (1835-1909) was the first great Romanian teacher of gymnastics. He began his career in Cluj, after which he worked for a long time in Bucharest. He translated a number of studies and papers on gymnastics from German into Romanian and founded many gymnastics associations in Transylvania and the Banat, as well as in Bucharest. Moceanu strongly advocated the introduction of gymnastics in the school curriculum and in army drills, writing, for this purpose, the first gymnastics textbooks and guides. Besides being a gymnast, he was also an excellent dancer and promoter of Romanian folk dancing, both in the country and abroad. The sport of gymnastics in Romania owes him a great deal.

Another great gymnastics teacher was Nicolae Velescu, a student and then colleague of Moceanu. He co-wrote studies and helped organize demonstrative tours of gymnastics and Romanian folk dances in the Far East. Dimitrie Ionescu (1864-1946) was another great personality and teacher of Romanian gymnastics. A graduate of the Central School of Gymnastics in Rome, in March 1892 he founded the magazine *The Romanian Gymnast,* which, beginning in 1907, became the official news bulletin of the Romanian Gymnastics Federation.

In 1910, the president of the Romanian Gymnastics Federation became a member of the board of the European Gymnastics Federation. Gymnastics continued to gain popularity in Romania. The year 1914 saw the founding of new associations in Aiud, Buzău, Lugoj, and Alexandria. The following year, in 1915, the ninth Congress of the Romanian Gymnastics Federation took place; on this occasion, King Ferdinand I issued a royal decree giving the federation full juridical authority.

Women began taking part in gymnastics programs between 1916 and 1932, as they competed in international competitions held in France, Italy, Yugoslavia, and Czechoslovakia. National tournaments, actual gymnastics festivals, continued to be organized in the country at regular intervals. In 1932 the Romanian Gymnastics Federation joined the Union of Sports Federations of Romania.

The period up to 1946 was characterized by the implementation and growth of the Swedish gymnastics system developed by Pierre Ling in schools, universities, the army, and at the National Academy of Physical Education. This was a direct result of many gymnastics specialists' being educated in Stockholm at the time.

With the installation of the communist regime in Romania at the end of World War II, the Soviet system gave a more formal quality to apparatus gymnastics, and it began to enter educational institutions as well as clubs. In 1947, the first national individual championships were organized in Reşita, while in 1950 Bucharest hosted the first school national championships. Several bilateral international competitions were also held between 1950 and 1951.

In the interval between 1950 and 1964, under the guidance of such great coaches as Iosif Maier, Adina Stroescu, Robert Podlaha, Nicolae Bălaşu, Caius Jianu, Petre Dungaciu, Maria Simionescu, and others, Romanian sports gymnastics saw a rapid development both from a technical and methodological point of view, as well as through the formation of many skilled specialists, some of whom are still actively working in Romanian gymnastics today.

The 1952 Helsinki Olympic Games saw the participation of the first Romanian Women's and Men's teams coming from Romania, although they performed modestly. The first national university championships took place in Arad in 1953, and the national champion was no other than the current president of the Romanian Gymnastics Federation, Nicolae

Vieru. This championship continued until 1980, when financial difficulties brought it to an end.

In Bucharest, in May 1957, the Romanian Gymnastics Federation organized the first European Women's Championships. The Romanian gymnasts Sonia Ivan and Elena Leuștean won the silver and bronze medals respectively at this event. Since 1956 a true rehearsal for the annual European Championships has been held under the name "the Romanian International Gymnastics Championships." It is the oldest individual world competition for both men and women, which this year celebrates its 40th anniversary.

The 1956 Melbourne Olympics, the 1958 World Championships in Moscow, and the 1960 Rome Olympics, each brought bronze medals for the Romanian Women's Gymnastics Team. Throughout the period from 1950 to 1964, both the Romanian men's and women's teams gained a great deal of experience in both Balkan, European, and World competitions, winning occasional medals.

The 1964 Tokyo Olympics saw poor results for Romania's teams, fourth place for the women and twelfth place for the men, a fact that nearly led Romanian officials of the time to cancel preparations for participation at the 1968 Olympic Games in Mexico City. Instead, a number of initiatives were undertaken to improve competitive Romanian gymnastics, efforts that began to bear fruit beginning in 1971-1972. These included temporary contacts with coaches from the Soviet Union and Japan. Romanian coaches were sent to study abroad and joint training was organized with the Soviet and Japanese teams. In 1969, the famous gymnastics school at Onești was created, a stronghold for women's gymnastics training.

Since 1961, national championships for rhythmic gymnastics have also been held, the efforts of the Federation in this respect bearing fruit in international competitions and continental and world championships. Starting with 1965, Romania regularly participated in the "Friendship" competition, a competition among socialist bloc countries. This competition launched the careers of many famous World and Olympic champions. In 1973, this competition was won by Nadia Comăneci.

At the 1972 Olympic Games in Munich the Romanian Women's Gymnastics Team came in fourth, while the men's team placed seventh. In 1973, the efforts made to improve the Romanian gymnastics program during the previous years bore fruit at the European

Dan Grecu

Championships. In London, Alina Goreac won the silver medal on the balance beam and the bronze medal on the floor exercise, while

23

Anca Grigoraş earned a bronze medal on the balance beam. In Grenoble, Dan Grecu won a silver medal on the rings. A year later, at the 1974 World Championships at Varna, Dan Grecu earned the first Romanian gold medal in an international competition on the rings, while the men's team came in sixth, and the women's fourth. Nadia Comăneci and the other juniors watched Dan Grecu from the audience.

Since 1975 the brilliant epoch of Romanian gymnastics, bearing the name of **Nadia Comăneci,** began. Born on 2 November 1961 in Oneşti, she began her training under Marcel Duncan (presently in Israel), who selected her. A gymnasium was built in Oneşti, in 1968, where the above mentioned school would be established the next year — centered mainly on gymnastics and supervised by Maria and George Simionescu.

For a year Nadia was trained by Valeriu Munteanu and Martha Karolyi, the latter fresh from Petroşani. At that time Bela Karolyi was working at a handball center.

Since 1971, the couple Martha and Bela coached Nadia, making her "the great Nadia," the queen of Montreal, a legend of world gymnastics, a fascinating personality that radically marked the period 1975-1981 in world gymnastics. Nadia took part in two Olympiads and won nine Olympic medals — five gold, three silver, and one bronze.

After the Montreal Olympics in 1976, Nicolae Ceauşescu, the president of the country,

Nadia Comăneci

awarded her the highest prize in communist Romania, "Hero of Socialist Labor."

Nadia also earned 4 World Championship medals (at Strasbourg in 1978 and Fort Worth in 1979), of which two were gold and two silver. As for the European championships, Nadia's record is unmatched: three times in succession absolute European champion (1975, 1977, and 1979), also winning the Challenge Cup. In addition, she achieved 9 gold and 3 silver medals. With her participation in the 1982 University Games held in Bucharest, where she won 4 gold medals, Nadia practically was bowing out of the arena. Her official retirement from competitive gymnastics was celebrated in May 1983, in Bucharest, honored by the presence of Juan Antonio Samaranch, Chairman of the International Olympic Committee, who awarded her, on this occasion, the Olympic lavaliere with silver laurels.

Nadia graduated from the Physical Education and Sports Institute in Bucharest and between 1983-1989 she worked for the Romanian Gymnastics Federation as a juniors' coach. Her fame and unparalleled popularity were begrudged by the Ceauşescus. On 25 November 1989, as a prelude to the imminent revolution that led to the overthrow of the communist regime, she left Romania, crossing the border illegally, living for a while in Canada, before settling in the United States. The major reasons for her leaving the country were the lack of individual freedom and the restrictions on traveling abroad that characterized the communist regime.

After a five year absence, Nadia returned to Romania and was given a well-deserved triumphant welcome throughout the country, at all levels, in Bucharest, Oneşti, and Deva. Her former school was also renamed in her honor. She returned to her native country again in April 1996 to exchange marriage vows with former American gymnastics star Bart Conner.

The 1976 Olympic Games in Montreal, Canada, relaunched Romanian gymnastics and had a decisive impact on the evolution of international gymnastics as well. Little girls the world over dreamed of becoming like Nadia. In Montreal, Nadia received the first perfect score ever awarded in Olympic history, repeating her feat of perfection seven times. She also won three gold medals, including the individual all-around title. Her teammate Teodora Ungureanu also impressed spectators with her performances,

Nadia and Teodora

winning a silver medal on the parallel bars and a bronze medal on the balance beam, and placing fourth in the individual all-around competition.

During the period from 1973 to 1975, Bela Karolyi had a colleague in Oneşti, the technician Iosif Hedi, lecturer at the

Gymnastics Department of the Institute of Physical Education, who had an important influence on Bela Karolyi's development as a coach. In the fall of 1977, at the request of Bela Karolyi, the center for women's gymnastics training moved from Oneşti to Deva. In a short time, conditions in Deva proved far superior to those in Oneşti, and the quality of training improved in direct proportion.

Deva Training Center

In the interval from 1977 to 1981, when the women's team was trained in Deva, Nadia and her colleagues obtained further successes. Namely, at the European Championships in Prague, which unfortunately ended with the withdrawal of the Romanian team at the orders of the dictator Ceauşescu, who deemed that Nadia had been wronged in her score on the vault. Mention should also be made of the excellent results obtained at the World Championships in Strasbourg in 1978, the European Championship in Copenhagen in 1979, and the World Championships in Fort Worth, Texas, in 1979, when the Romanian women's team won the world title for the first time. At this championship, Nadia was able to participate only in the compulsories and on the beam, as she had a severe infection in her left hand. Nadia's score on the beam was sufficient for Romania to surpass the formidable team of the Soviet Union and to obtain the world title by 0.65 points. In addition, Romanian gymnasts won two world titles: Emilia Eberle on the floor exercise and Dumitriţa Turner on the vault.

Emilia Eberle

The 1980 Olympic Games in Moscow, boycotted by Western countries because of the Soviet invasion of Afghanistan, brought Romania seven medals — two gold, three silver, and two bronze medals. Unfortunately, the gymnastics competition was tarnished by a judging controversy surrounding Nadia Comăneci's performance on the balance beam that resulted in her winning only the silver medal in the individual all-around competition.

Between 1977 and 1980 Nadia went through two short periods of time without the benefit of Bela Karolyi's training. The latter's demanding training regime and Nadia's reaching her limits professionally and personally caused some difficulties. Nevertheless, they worked together and achieved success at both the Strasbourg and Moscow competitions.

Nadia and the Romanian team, led by coach Bela Karolyi, went on a successful demonstration tours throughout the United States, Mexico, and Venezuela. During the last tour, in 1981, in the United States, Bela Karolyi defected for political reasons. This shocked the public at large and communist leader Nicolae Ceauşescu in particular. The Romanian Gymnastics Federation itself faced a difficult time as no assistant coach had been close enough to Karolyi, who might now take his place.

During these years, the Romanian men's team trained at the Bucharest center. The team maintained a leading position in the world standings, relying heavily on the results obtained by Dan Grecu, who earned bronze medals in Montreal and Strasbourg and a silver medal at the World Championships at Fort Worth in 1979. At the 1980 Moscow Olympic Games, however, he suffered a torn muscle that was to mark the end of his career.

Ecaterina Szabo

Ecaterina Szabo and Simona Păucă

Meanwhile, the Deva center carried on with a group of younger coaches and several talented young gymnasts from throughout the country. The new women's coach, Octavian Belu, proved himself to be a worthy successor to Karolyi. As a result the Romanian women's gymnastics program continued to improve and to obtain excellent results on the international level. Thus, at the World Championships in Budapest in 1983, the 1984 Los Angeles Olympic Games, the 1985 World Championships in Montreal, the 1987 World Championships in Rotterdam, the 1989 World Championships in Stuttgart, and at the Olympic Games in Seoul in 1988, as well as at the European Championships at Goteborg (1983), Helsinki (1985), Moscow (1987), and Brussels (1989), the Romanian women's team surpassed even previous results.

The whole gymnastics world foresaw ruin for Romania after Bela Karolyi's departure, yet resources for its continuation were found. Gymnasts such as Ecaterina Szabo, Daniela Silivaş, Aurelia Dobre, Lavinia Agache, Simona Păucă, and Laura Cutina proved to be brilliant successors to Nadia Comăneci.

At the 1984 Olympic Games in Los Angeles, the Romanian team received a standing ovation from the American public as it was the only country to defy the Soviet-led boycott of the games. Led by Ecaterina Szabo, the Romanian Women's Gymnastics Team won its first Olympic championship.

In 1987 Aurelia Dobre became the first Romanian gymnast to win the individual

Aurelia Dobre

allaround title at the World Championships in Rotterdam. At the Olympic Games in Seoul, South Korea, the following year, Daniela Silivaş dominated the women's gymnastics competition. Silivaş brought home an impressive six Olympic medals: gold medals on the parallel bars, balance beam, and floor exercise; silver medals in the team competition and individual all-around competition; and a bronze medal on the vault.

From 1983 to the present the Romanian men's gymnastics team has been training in Reşita, while the juniors train in Timişoara. They have also obtained good results. Marius Gherman, Marian Rizan, Kurt Szilier, Marius Tobă, and Nicu Pascu are among the best male gymnasts.

Romanian rhythmic gymnastics had its brightest moment at the 1984 Olympic Games in Los Angeles, where Doina Stănculescu won the silver medal.

Daniela Silivaş

The December 1989 Revolution that saw the overthrow of the communist regime in Romania also brought some changes to the gymnastics program — both at the level of the Federation and down to the local clubs things have been reorganized on a democratic basis. Political authorities no longer interfere in sports. Rhythmic gymnastics has split from the Federation and formed their own, independent federation.

Since 1989, the women's training center in Deva and the men's center in Reşiţa have received increased support and an influx of new athletes and coaches. The principal coaches, Dan Grecu for the men's team and Octavian Belu for the women's team, are in large measure responsible for the continued success of the Romanian Gymnastics Federation. As a result of their efforts, remarkable results have been seen between 1990 and 1995. Romanian gymnastics registered great successes at the 1991 World Championships in Indianapolis, the 1992 Olympic Games at Barcelona, and the World Championships in Birmingham in 1993. The Olympic Games in Barcelona were highlighted by Lavinia Miloşovici's gold medal winning performances on the vault and floor exercise. At the World Championships in Dortmund, Germany, in 1994, and Sabae, Japan, in 1995, the women's team won two successive world titles. The stars of Romanian gymnastics during this period have been Cristina Bontaş, Mirela Paşca, Lavinia Miloşovici, Gina Gogean, Simona Amânar, and Alexandra Marinescu.

Dortmund Team

The Romanian male gymnasts have also obtained hitherto unheard of successes, winning gold and bronze medals in Brisbane — Marius Urzică on the pommel horse and Dan Burincă on the rings. At the 1995 World Championships in Sabae, the men's team placed third, a well-deserved achievement.

Gina Gogean

The 1994 Stockholm European Championships and the 1996 Birmingham European Championships were dominated by Romanian women gymnasts, both seniors and juniors.

The Romanian Gymnastics Federation is amply represented in all international organizations. Romanian experts of repute play vital roles in the International Gymnastics Federation and European Gymnastics Union. Since 1972 Maria Simionescu has been deputy-chair of the technical feminine committee of the International Gymnastics Federation. Since 1976 Nicolae Vieru has been a member of the executive committee of the International Gymnastics Federation, while Adrian Stoica has been, since 1992, deputy chairman of the men's technical committee of the International Gymnastics Federation. Anca Grigoraş is also a member of the women's technical committee of the European Gymnastics Union.

At the individual apparatus World Championships in San Juan, Puerto Rico in 1996, on the eve of the Olympic Games in Atlanta, Georgia, in the United States, the Romanian team continued its string of impressive performances, highlighted by Gina Gogean's gold medal winning routines on the vault and floor exercise. With the centennial edition of the Olympic Games set to begin, the outlook for the future of Romanian gymnastics and of the Romanian Gymnastics Federation is bright.

Gymnast Alexandra Marinescu training for the 1996 Olympic Games

THE 1996 ROMANIAN WOMEN'S GYMNASTICS TEAM

The 1996 Romanian Women's Gymnastics Team enters the centennial edition of the Olympic Games as two-time world champions. The strength and long-term consistency of the Romanian gymnastics program can be attributed in large measure to the dedication and skill of Coach Octavian Belu and the support received from the Romanian Gymnastics Federation under President Nicolae Vieru. With the help of his assistant coaches, Maria Bitang, Nicolae Forminte, Benone Pereţeanu, Toma Ponoran, and Doina Olaru, Coach Belu has prepared a team of talented young gymnasts who hope to continue their success of the past two years at the Olympic Games in Atlanta.

OCTAVIAN BELU

Octavian Belu has been the coach of the Romanian Women's Gymnastics Team since the defection of Bela Karolyi from Romania for political reasons in 1981. A native of Ploieşti, Belu took over a program that most experts considered would falter after the loss of Karolyi, and not only continued its outstanding success, but improved upon it. As a result, he has become the most successful gymnastics coach in the world, training numerous world champions and leading the Romanian team to victory in the past two world championships. His dedication and commitment to excellence have meant the key to success for Romanian gymnastics.

Belu started out in gymnastics as an athlete. He also played volleyball and basketball and took up diving. A mediocre gymnast by his own admission, he was all the more driven to study the technical aspects of the sport, methodology, and training. In 1974 he graduated from the Faculty of Physical Education and Sports Institute in Bucharest. He worked for a time as a teacher of Physical Education at Valea Călugărească before returning to Ploieşti where he began coaching gymnastics. He is married. His wife Camelia works as a nurse in Ploieşti, and he has one daughter, Iolanda, who is eighteen.

On the eve of the 1996 Olympic Games in Atlanta, Octavian Belu agreed to answer a few questions for this book:

How does the situation of Romanian Gymnastics today differ from that up to 1989?

The international balance of gymnastics has changed with the disappearance of the Soviet Union as a world power. Instead of having to compete against a strong team with vast human and material resources, this has now been broken up into several smaller teams, dispersing the conglomeration of talent and resources that made the Soviet gymnastics program so powerful. In addition, we have seen the rise of China as a world power in women's gymnastics.

As for the Romanian program, except for the brief period in 1990 when the national training center in Deva was closed, we have managed to preserve our traditional system and avoid hazardous experiments. It is important that we preserve those elements which have brought success to Romanian gymnastics and which have become to be imitated throughout the world, especially in the United States after the arrival of Bela Karolyi.

In addition, the changes in Romanian society after the collapse of the communist regime have also impacted gymnastics. Relationship between coaches and athletes are changing. The rapid changes that have gone on in Romanian society have led to some confusion among the youth about the meaning of freedom and liberty. At times, relations with the families of the athletes have become more difficult. As the financial element has begun to enter into gymnastics, parents have become more pretentious and some object to the rigorous training schedule. Still, we have been very lucky and have managed to preserve a family atmosphere in Deva. Athletes are now allowed to keep the prizes they win in international competitions and, as a result, receive some financial renumeration for their efforts.

Still, more money is needed in the Romanian gymnastics program. Many clubs lack money for medicine, travel expenses, and to purchase equipment. The Romanian Gymnastics Federation, under President Nicolae Vieru, has made great efforts, but it does not have sufficient resources and needs private sponsorship to improve the situation. The majority of expenses are still paid from the state budget, but at least the possibility for sponsorship exists. A serious problem has been the fact that many coaches have left the country because of the economic situation. It is hard for them to resist the offers of better pay from clubs in foreign countries.

Of the many great gymnasts whom you trained in the past, who were the most talented?

I would say that the gymnast who best fulfilled all the characteristics of a true champion was Daniela Silivaş, together with Ecaterina Szabo. Each generation of gymnasts seems to have two leaders. First there was Nadia Comăneci and Teodora Ungureanu, then Ecaterina Szabo and Lavinia Agache, followed by Ecaterina Szabo and Aurelia Dobre, after them came Daniela Silivaş and Cristina Bontaş, and, at present, the team leaders are Lavinia Miloşovici and Gina Gogean.

How are the girls selected for the national team and what is their normal training schedule?

Most of the girls are selected in school usually during the first grade. There are four or five stages in the selection process and usually by the fifth grade they are filtered out through a series of local competitions and selections. Some of the girls are encouraged by their parents to try out for gymnastics. The normal training program for the girls at the national training center is six hours daily: three hours in the morning and three hours in the evening.

What special measures have you taken to prepare for the Olympic Games in Atlanta?

We have basically remained with our traditional training program that has brought us the successful results we have obtained to date. One thing we did do was to acquire American equipment (parallel bars, balance beam, and vault) for our training center in Deva as these apparatuses differ somewhat from European equipment and we wanted our girls to be able to become acquainted with the conditions they will confront in Atlanta.

How do you see the prospects for the Romanian team at the 1996 Olympic Games in Atlanta?

Judging from the results we have obtained during the past two years, I am optimistic. We have excellent chances for a team medal and for individual medals. The most important thing is for our gymnasts to be healthy. Many of them have minor injuries resulting from the too rigorous competition schedule, something that international gymnastics officials need to analyze.

In the team competition, I believe that it will be a struggle between us, the United States, Russia, and China. Since 1991, our best gymnast is Lavinia Miloşovici and we have high hopes for her in the all-around competition and on the floor exercise. She is a strong gymnast and a true team leader and, if she is healthy, she should have remarkable success in Atlanta. In addition, we

have a number of younger gymnasts with great potential who will be contenders for individual medals: Gina Gogean on the vault and floor exercise, Simona Amânar on the vault, and Alexandra Marinescu on the balance beam and parallel bars.

We also have an excellent coaching staff: Maria Bitang from Oneşti, former juniors' trainer, coaches the balance beam; Nicolae Forminte from Constanţa coaches the vault; Benone Pereţeanu from Bucharest coaches the uneven parallel bars, together with Toma Ponoran from Oneşti; our choreographer is Doina Olaru from Ploieşti. I have generally coached the floor exercise.

Atlanta will mark the end of an era for gymnastics. After the Olympics, the minimum age will rise to sixteen, there will be scoring changes, and there will be no more compulsories. In the future, gymnastics will have to struggle to maintain its individual identity so as not to become too much like rhythmic gymnastics or to become a circus show. A balance must be maintained and this must be carefully thought out by the International Gymnastics Federation.

Lavinia Milosovici

LAVINIA MILOŞOVICI

Born in Lugoj on 21 October 1976, Lavinia Corina Miloşovici is the leading Romanian gymnast of the 1990s, having won numerous international titles. The daughter of Tănase and Iltiko Miloşovici, Lavinia began gymnastics at the age of six, after being selected for the training center in Deva. She has one brother, Cristian, who is twenty-one years old, and her family currently lives in Orşova.

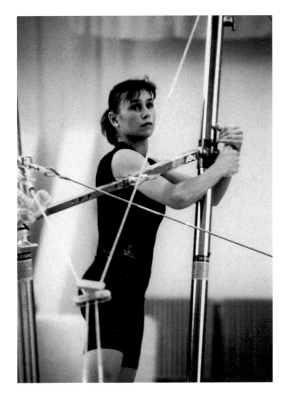

Lavinia's favorite gymnast is Nadia Comăneci who inspired her to take up the sport. Her favorite apparatuses are the vault and the floor exercise. Lavinia finished high school last year. Her favorite subjects in school were Romanian and Biology. Although she has no plans to stop performing, when she retires from gymnastics, Lavinia hopes to become a gymnastics

trainer and a judge. At the 1992 Olympic Games in Barcelona, Spain, she won a bronze medal in the individual all-around competition, and gold medals on the vault and floor exercise.

Her hobbies include music and movies. She likes detective movies and action films and her favorite actor is Jean Claude van Damme. Lavinia's favorite food is French fries. Of the places she has visited, Lavinia likes Italy, France, Japan, and the United States the most. The leader of the Romanian women's gymnastics team, she has high hopes for the 1996 Olympic Games in Atlanta. At 19 years old, Lavinia is 5'1" tall and weighs 108 pounds. When asked to address the American public watching the gymnastics competition at the Olympic Games, Lavinia replied, "I want to thank all of my fans in America for their support and I hope that they will take the time to learn more about my country."

GINA GOGEAN

Born on 9 September 1977, Gina Gogean is one of the biggest stars of Romanian gymnastics, having won numerous international titles. She was born in a small village called Câmpuri, near Focşani, in the county of Vrancea. Her father, Emil, is a driving instructor, and her mother, Anica, is a factory worker. She has one sister, Maricica, who is a medical student at the University of Iaşi.

Gina began gymnastics at the age of six. Her favorite apparatuses are the vault and the floor exercise and her favorite gymnasts include Nadia Comăneci and Daniela Silivaş. When she finishes gymnastics she hopes to become a coach.

Gina's hobbies include music and watching television. Her favorite singer is Michael Jackson and her favorite actor is Eddie Murphy. In her spare time, Gina also likes to read adventure novels and shop for clothes.

Her favorite subject in school is Biology. Of the cities she has visited, Rome, with its many ancient historical monuments, is her favorite.

In addition to team success, Gina's goal is to obtain an individual medal at the 1996 Olympic Games in Atlanta. At age 18, Gina is 4'11" tall and weighs 88 pounds. When asked if she would like to say something to the Americans watching the gymnastics competition at the Olympic Games, Gina said, "I want to thank our fans in America for encouraging us and I hope that they will support us in the same way that they will support the American team."

Simona Amânar

SIMONA AMÂNAR

One of the brightest young stars of Romanian gymnastics, Simona Amânar was born on 7 October 1979 in Constanţa. The daughter of Vasile and Sofia Amânar, Simona's father is a

technician at a shipyard in Constanţa and her mother is a housewife. She has one brother, Adrian, who is fifteen. Simona began gymnastics at the age of six in Constanţa. In 1992 she moved to the national training center in Deva, together with her coach, Nicolae Forminte, who is now an assistant coach for the national team. Her favorite apparatus is the vault and her favorite gymnasts include Camelia Voinea, Daniela Silivaş, and Shannon Miller. Simona's greatest success in international competition to date came at the 1995 World Championships in Sabae, Japan, where she won the gold medal in the vault and placed fourth in the individual all-around competition.

In her spare time, Simona likes to read and to watch movies. She likes adventure novels and science fiction books. Her favorite actor is Jean Claude van Damme. In school, Simona's favorite subject is Romanian. Of the places that she has had the opportunity to visit, one of her favorites is Walt Disney Land in the United States.

Simona has a great deal of promise and looks forward to the challenge that the Olympic Games present. At 16 years old, she is 4'9" tall and weighs 77 pounds. Her message to the American public at the Olympic Games in Atlanta is "I hope that you will support and encourage me at the Games."

Alexandra Marinescu

ALEXANDRA MARINESCU

One of the best young Romanian gymnasts and a bright hope in Atlanta, Alexandra Marinescu was born in Bucharest on 19 March 1981. Her mother, Anca, is a computer analyst, and her father, Alexandru, is a quality controller at a factory in Bucharest.

She began gymnastics in Bucharest at the age of four, at the suggestion of her swimming instructor who noticed that she might have an aptitude for gymnastics. Her favorite apparatus is the balance beam and her favorite gymnasts are Cristina Bontaş, Nadia Comăneci, and Lavinia Miloşovici.

She came to the national training center in Deva at the beginning of 1996, together with her coach Benone Pereţeanu, who is now an assistant coach with the national team.

One of her brightest moments was at the 1996 World Championships in San Juan, Puerto Rico, where she won the silver medal on the balance beam.

In her spare time, Alexandra likes to read and to listen to music. She especially likes adventure novels and science fiction books. She also likes watching comedy movies and her favorite actors are Tom Hanks and Jim Carey. Alexandra also loves chocolate. In school, her favorite subjects are Mathematics, Art, and English. Of the places she has visited so far, her favorite is Stockholm, Sweden.

Alexandra hopes to win both team and individual medals at the 1996 Olympic Games in Atlanta. At the age of 15, she is 4'10" tall and weighs 79 pounds. To the fans at the Olympic Games, Alexandra says, "I hope that Americans watching the Romanian gymnastics team at the Olympics will want to learn more about my country."

Annamaria Bean

ANAMARIA BICAN

A talented young gymnast, Anamaria Bican was born in Zărneşti, in the county of Braşov, on 3 March 1980. Her father, Grigore, is an engineer and her mother, ştefana, works in a chemical laboratory. She has two brothers, Ioan, who is eighteen, and Cătălin, who is eleven.

Anamaria began gymnastics at the age of six in Oneşti. Her favorite apparatus is the vault and her favorite gymnasts include the Russian gymnast Oksana Fabrishinova and her teammate Gina Gogean.

She came to the national training center in Deva in 1993, together with her coach Toma Ponoran, who is now an assistant coach with the national team. Anamaria's hobbies include reading and playing electronic games. She likes detective stories and her favorite author is Agatha Christie. Her favorite subject in school is Mathematics.

Of the places that she has had the opportunity to visit, Anamaria was most impressed by the Vatican City.
A rising star of Romanian gymnastics, Anamaria hopes to win an Olympic medal in Atlanta. At sixteen years old, she is 5'0" tall and weighs 81 pounds. Anamaria's message to the public at the Olympic Games: "I want to thank the American public at the Olympic Games for their support during the competition."

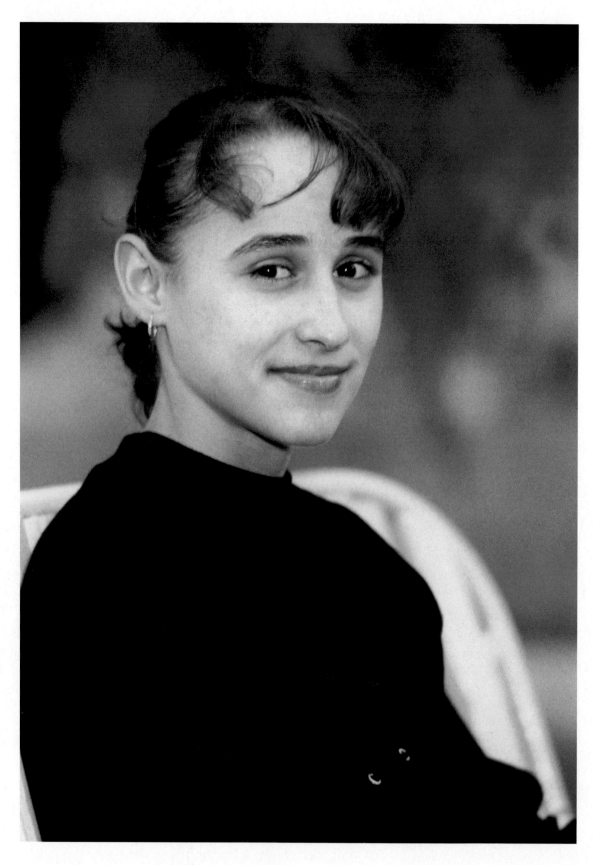

Tonela Looies

IONELA LOAIEŞ

A member of the team that won the 1994 World Championship in Dortmund, Germany, Ionela Loaieş was born in Comăneşti, near Bacău, on 1 February 1979. Her father, Ion, is a miner and her mother, Elena, works in a furniture factory. She has one brother, Marius, age twenty.

Ionela began gymnastics at the age of six in Oneşti. Her favorite apparatuses are the parallel bars and the floor exercise and her favorite gymnasts are Nadia Comăneci and teammates Gina Gogean and Lavinia Miloşovici.

Ionela's hobbies are reading, watching television, listening to music, and playing electronic games. She likes detective stories and her favourite singer is Michael Jackson. Her favorite actor is Steven Segal.

Her preferred food is the traditional Romanian dish *sarmale* (stuffed cabbage). In school, Ionela's favorite subject is English. Of the cities she has visited, Chicago is her favorite.

One of the talented young gymnasts on the Romanian National team, at age 17, Ionela is 4'10" tall and weighs 84 pounds. Her message to those watching the gymnastics competition in Atlanta is: "I hope that the American public will support and encourage us at the Olympic Games."

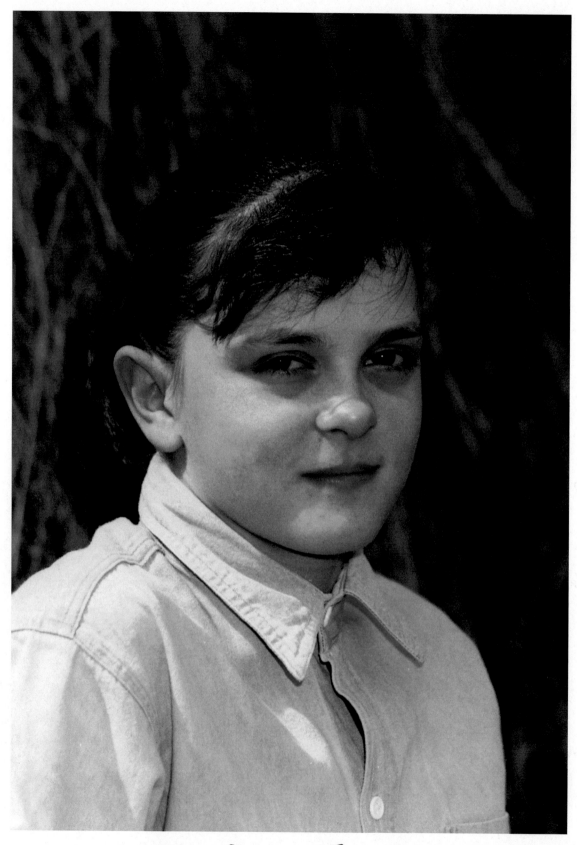

Mirela Tyurlan

MIRELA ȚUGURLAN

A bright young star of Romanian gymnastics, Mirela Țugurlan (pronounced *Tsugurlan*) was born in Focșani on 4 September 1980. Her father, Marinică, is an auto mechanic and her mother, Frosa, is a seamstress. She has one brother, Daniel, who is seventeen.

She began gymnastics at the age of eight. Her favorite apparatus is the parallel bars and her favorite gymnasts are Nadia Comăneci and teammates Lavinia Miloșovici and Gina Gogean. When she finishes competing, her goal is to become a gymnastics coach.

Mirela's hobbies are reading horror stories and watching horror movies. She also likes to go shopping for cosmetics. Her favorite subjects in school are Physics and Chemistry. Of the places she has visited, her favorite city is Atlanta.

A talented Romanian gymnast with a promising future, at age 15 Mirela is 4'7" tall and weighs 79 pounds. When asked to address the American public watching the Olympic Games, Mirela answered, "I want to tell the American people that I love them and I hope that they will support and encourage me in Atlanta."

Claudia Presăcan

CLAUDIA PRESĂCAN

A member of the team that won the 1994 and 1995 World Championships, Claudia Maria Presăcan was born in Sibiu on 28 December 1979. Her father, Adrian, is a veterinary technician and her mother, Eugenia, is a housewife. She has two brothers, Claudiu, age fourteen, and Cristian, age ten, and one sister, Alina, age six.

Claudia began gymnastics at the age of seven and her favorite apparatus is the balance beam. Her favorite gymnast is Nadia Comăneci.

In her free time, Claudia enjoys reading and listening to music. She also likes to watch action and detective movies. In school, her favorite subject is English. Among the cities she has visited, Claudia was most impressed by Sabae in Japan.

A bright, young star of Romanian gymnastics, at age 16 Claudia is 4'10" tall and weighs 79 pounds. Her message to the American public in Atlanta is: "I hope that they will support us and I want to wish them all good health and success in life."

Alexandra Dobrescu

ALEXANDRA DOBRESCU

One of the talented new young gymnasts on the Romanian national team, Alexandra "Anda" Ionela Dobrescu was born in Târgoviște on 2 May 1980. Her parents are Eugeniu Iona and Tea Valeria Dobrescu. Her father manages a sports complex in Târgoviște and her mother is a housewife. She has two brothers, eighteen year-old Marian and twenty-two year-old Laurenţiu who is a student in electronics at the University of Bucharest, and one sister, Valentina, who is nineteen.

Anda began gymnastics at the age of seven. Her favorite apparatus is the floor exercise and her favorite gymnasts are Nadia Comăneci and Lavinia Miloşovici. When she finishes competing, Anda wants to become a gymnastics coach.

Her hobbies are listening to music and learning to speak English. She also likes to read detective stories. Her favorite subjects in school are Romanian and English and her favorite Romanian writer is the national poet Mihai Eminescu. Of the places she has visited, Anda was most impressed with Rome and the Vatican City.

A young gymnast, with excellent prospects, at age 16 Anda is 4'7" tall and weighs 77 pounds. Her message for spectators in Atlanta: "I want to thank the American people for their reception and I would like to invite them to visit Romania."

Andreq Cacoran

ANDREEA CACOVEAN

Born in Turda, in the county of Cluj, on 15 September 1978, Andreea Cacovean is one of the bright stars of the new generation of Romanian gymnasts. The daughter of Mircea and Ana Maria Cacovean, who are both hydrological technicians, Andreea has two brothers: Andrei, age 20, who is a student in electronics at the University of Cluj, and Mircea, who is 15.

She began gymnastics at the age of seven, being selected for the national training center in Deva. Her favorite apparatus is the parallel bars and her favorite gymnasts include Nadia Comăneci, Ecaterina Szabo, and her teammates Lavinia Miloşovici and Gina Gogean.

Andreea's hobbies include reading and listening to music. She likes to read detective stories and also to watch action movies. Her favorite subjects in school include Mathematics and English, which she speaks very well. Her favorite foods are French fries and ice cream. Of the countries she has visited thus far, Andreea likes the Netherlands the best.

A talented, young Romanian gymnast, at age 17 Andreea is 4'9" tall and weighs 77 pounds. Her message to those watching the Olympic Games is: "I hope that the American public will receive us with hospitality and give equal support to athletes from all countries."

ROMANIAN GYMNASTICS AT THE OLYMPIC GAMES

SUMMARY OF RESULTS

Helsinki, 1952

Team, Women

9th Place: Romania (25. Stela Perim 71.85; 52. Olga Gölner 70.07; 58. Ileana Gyarfaş 69.61; 68. Olga Munteanu 69.00; 79. Helga Bârsan 68.00; 85. Eveline Slavici 67.73) 482.06.

Team, Men

20th Place: Romania (71. Frederic Orendi 105.05; 124. Mihail Botez 98.20; 157. Francisc Kociş 88.80; 161. Eugen Balint 88.60; 165. Carol Bedö 87.20; Aurel Loşniţă 85.65) 499.85.

Melbourne, 1956

Team, Women

3rd Place: Romania (Elena Leuşteanu, Sonia Iovan, Emilia Vătăşoiu-Liţă, Ileana Săcălici, Utta Schland-Porceanu, Elena Dobrovolschi, Georgeta Hurumuzachi) 364.80.

Individual All-Around, Women

4th Place: Elena Leuşteanu 74.366

Apparatus Finals, Women

Floor Exercise, 3rd Place: Elena Leuşteanu 18.699; Balance Beam, 6th Place: Elena Leuşteanu 18.500; Vault, 6th Place: Elena Leuşteanu 18.632; Parallel Bars, 10th Place: Elena Leuşteanu 18.532.

Rome, 1960

Team, Women

3rd Place: Romania (Sonia Iovan, Elena Leuşteanu, Atanasia Ionescu, Emilia Liţă, Elena Dobrovolschi, Utta Schland-Poreceanu) 372.053.

Individual All-Around, Women

5th Place: Sonia Iovan 75.797.

Tokyo, 1964

Team, Women

6th Place: Romania (14. Sonia Iovan 75.397; 20. Elena Leuşteanu 75.130; 37. Elena Ceampelea 73.831; 41. Atanasia Ionescu 73.698; 48. Emilia Liţă 72.995; 54. Cristina Doboşan 72.497) 371.984.

Team, Men

12th Place: Romania (31. Frederic Orendi 111.40; 40. Gheorghe Tobăneanu 110.60; 51. Anton Cadar 110.45; 69. Alexandru. Silaghi 109.65; 86. Gheorghe Condovici 107.15; 88. Petre Miclăuş 107.10) 550.65.

München, 1972

Team, Women

6th Place: Romania (Elena Ceampelea 73.05; Alina Goreac 72.25; Anca Grigoraş 72.10; Elisabeta Turcu 71.20; Paula Ioan 71.10; Marcela Păunescu 70.50) 360.70.

Individual All-Around, Women

22nd Place: Elena Ceampelea 73.375; 29th Place: Anca Grigoraş 72.850; 31st Place: Alina Goreac 72.825.

Team, Men

7th Place: Romania (Petre Mihaiuc 109.30; Dan Grecu 108.10; Gheorghe Păunescu 107.25; Mircea Gheorghiu 105.00; Nicolae Oprescu 104.60; Constantin Petrescu 103.70) 538.90.

Individual All-Around, Men

32nd Place: Dan Grecu 108.850; 34th Place: Petre Mihaiuc 108.650.

Montreal, 1976

Team, Women

2nd Place: Romania (Gabriela Truşcă 76.10; Georgeta Gabor 75.70; Anca Grigoraş 76.70; Mariana Constantin 76.75; Teodora Ungureanu 78.05; Nadia Comăneci 79.05) 387.15.

Individual All-Around, Women

1st Place: Nadia Comăneci 79.275;
4th Place: Teodora Ungureanu 78.375;
11th Place: Mariana Constantin 76.625.

Apparatus Finals, Women

Vault, 4th Place: Nadia Comăneci;
Parallel Bars, 1st Place: Nadia Comăneci 20.00; 2nd Place: Teodora Ungureanu 19.800;
Balance Beam, 1st place: Nadia Comăneci 19.950; 3rd Place Teodora Ungureanu 19.700;
Floor Exercise, 3rd Place: Nadia Comăneci 19.750.

Team, Men

6th Place: Romania (48. ştefan Gal 109.15; 38. Mihai Borş 109.75; 36. Sorin Cepoi 109.95; 34. Nicolae Oprescu 110.30; Dan Grecu 114.10; 37. Ion Checicheş 109.85) 557.30.

Individual All-Around, Men

29th Place: Nicolae Oprescu 109.900;
32nd Place: Sorin Cepoi 109.525;
36th Place: Dan Grecu 60.450 (injured).

Apparatus Finals, Men

Rings, 3rd Place: Dan Grecu 19.500;
Vault, 4th Place: Dan Grecu 19.200.

Moscow, 1980

Team, Women

2nd Place: Romania (Nadia Comăneci 79.05; Rodica Dunca 78.50; Emilia Eberle 79.10; Melita Ruhn 78.30; Dumitriţa Turner 77.25; Cristina Grigoraş 78.00) 393.50.

Individual All-Around, Women

2nd Place: Nadia Comăneci 79.075;
6th Place: Emilia Eberle 78.400;
7th Place: Rodica Dunca 78.350.

Apparatus Finals, Women

Vault, 3rd Place: Melita Ruhn 19.650; 5th Place: Nadia Comăneci 19.350;
Parallel Bars, 2nd Place: Emilia Eberle 19.850; 3rd Place: Melita Ruhn 19.775;
Balance Beam, 1st Place: Nadia Comăneci 19.800; 6th Place: Emilia Eberle 19.400;
Floor Exercise, 1st Place: Nadia Comăneci 19,875; 5th Place: Emilia Eberle 19.750.

Team, Men

4th Place: Romania (Romulus Bucuroiu 112.75; Sorin Cepoi 113.55; Aurelian Georgescu 113.75; Dan Grecu 114.85; Nicolae Oprescu 112.95; Kurt Szilier 114.80) 572.30.

Individual All-Around, Men

9th Place: Dan Grecu 115.225;
14th Place: Kurt Szilier 114.650;
18th Place: Aurelian Georgescu 114.075.

Apparatus Finals, Men

Rings, 6th Place: Dan Grecu (injured) 10.850.

Los Angeles, 1984

Team, Women

1st Place: Romania (Ecaterina Szabo 39.375; Laura Cutina 39.200; Simona Păucă 39.025; Cristina Grigoraş 38.950; Mihaela Stănuleţ 38.850; Lavinia Agache 38.800) 392.20.

Individual All-Around, Women

2nd Place: Ecaterina Szabo 79.125;
3rd Place: Simona Păucă 78.675.

Apparatus Finals, Women

Vault, 1st Place: Ecaterina Szabo 19.875; 3rd Place: Lavinia Agache 19.750;
Parallel Bars, 4th Place: Mihaela Stănuleţ 19.650;
Balance Beam, 1st Place: Simona Păucă 19.800; 1st Place: Ecaterina Szabo 19.800;
Floor Exercise, 1st Place: Ecaterina Szabo 19.975; 8th Place: Laura Cutina 19.150.

Individual All-Around, Men

14th Place: Emilian Nicula 116.025;
15th Place: Valentin Pantea 116.00.

Apparatus Finals, Men

Floor Exercise, 6th Place: Valentin Pantea;
Rings, 7th Place: Emilian Nicula 19.500.

Rythmic Gymnastics, Individual All-Around

2nd Place: Doina Stăiculescu 57.900;
4th Place: Alina Drăgan.

Seoul, 1988

Team, Women

2nd Place: Romania (Camelia Voinea 77.775; Eugenia Golea 77.875; Celestina Popa 78.575; Gabriela Potorac 78.925; Daniela Silivaş 79.575; Aurelia Dobre 78.675) 394.125.

Individual All-Around, Women

2nd Place: Daniela Silivaş 79.637;
4th Place: Gabriela Potorac 79.037;
6th Place: Aurelia Dobre 78.812.

Apparatus Finals, Women

Vault, 2nd Place: Gabriela Potorac 19.830; 3rd Place: Daniela Silivaş 18.818;
Parallel Bars, 1st Place: Daniela Silivaş 20.00; 7th Place: Aurelia Dobre 19.824;
Balance Beam, 1st Place: Daniela Silivaş 19.924; 3rd Place: Gabriela Potorac 19.837;
Floor Exercise, 1st Place: Daniela Silivaş 19.937.

Team, Men

7th Place: Romania (Marian Rizan 114.85; Adrian Sandu 115.15; Nicolae Bejenaru 115.30; Marius Toba 116.75; Marius Gherman 117.55; Valentin Pântea 105.55) 581.70.

Individual All-Around, Men

5th Place: Marius Gherman 117.825;
21st Place: Marius Toba 115.400;
33rd Place: Nicolae Bejenaru 115.400.

Apparatus Finals, Men

Parallel Bars, 5th Place: Marius Gherman 19.700;
Horizontal Bar, 3rd Place: Marius Gherman 19.800.

Barcelona, 1992

Team, Women

2nd Place: Romania (Cristina Bontaş 79.211; Gina Gogean 78.886; Vanda Hădărean 78.761; Lavinia Miloşovici 79.198; Maria Neculiţă 78.623; Mirela Paşca 78.585) 395.079.

Individual All-Around, Women

3rd Place: Lavinia Miloşovici 39.687;
4th Place: Cristina Bontaş 39.674;
6th Place: Gina Gogean 39.624.

Apparatus Finals, Women

Vault, 1st Place: Lavinia Miloşovici 9.925; 5th Place: Gina Gogean 9.893;
Parallel Bars, 4th Place: Lavinia Miloşovici, Mirela Paşca 9.912;
Balance Beam, 4th Place: Cristina Bontaş; 8th Place: Lavinia Miloşovici 9.262;
Floor Exercise, 1st Place: Lavinia Miloşovici 10.00; 3rd Place: Cristina Bontaş 9.912.

Team, Men

7th Place: Romania (Nicolae Bejenaru 113.150; Adrian Gal 113.325; Marius Gherman 115.300; Marian Rizan 114.725; Adrian Sandu 112.850; Nicu Stroia 112.925) 571.150.

Individual All-Around, Men

7th Place: Marius Gherman 57.700;
20th Place: Adrian Gal 57.050;
30th Place: Marian Rizan 56.475.

ROMANIAN GYMNASTICS AT THE WORLD CHAMPIONSHIPS

SUMMARY OF RESULTS

Rome, 1954

Team, Women

    4th Place: Romania 498.57

Individual All-Around, Women

    5th Place: Elena Leuşteanu 74.24;
    19th Place: Agneta Hofman 71.97;
    33rd Place: Anita Ticu 70.53;
    42nd Place: Emilia Liţă 69.94;
    49th Place: Elena Dobrovolski 69.71;
    64th Place: Teofila Băiaşu 68.33;
    67th Place: Eveline Slavici 68.19.

Apparatus Finals, Women

    Balance Beam, 6th Place: Elena Leuşteanu 18.62.

Individual All-Around, Men

    62nd Place: Andrei Kerekes 103.45;
    67th Place: Frederic Orendi 102.35;
    109th Place: Mihai Botez 94.40.

Moscow, 1958

Team, Women

    3rd Place: Romania 367.020.

Individual All-Around, Women

    9th Place: Ileana Petroşanu 74.097;
    17th Place: Elena Leuşteanu 73.264;
    21st Place: Anastasia Ionescu 73.031;
    22nd Place: Sonia Ivan 72.997;
    31st Place: Emilia Liţă 72.498;
    57th Place: Elena Dobrovolschi 71.496.

Apparatus Finals, Women

    Vault, 6th Place: Elena Leuşteanu 18.799.

Team, Men

    13th Place: Romania 528.40.

Individual All-Around, Men

    20th Place: Frederic Orendi 109.20;
    79th Place: Ion Zamfir 103.80;
    81st Place: Andrei Kerekes 103.75;
    85th Place: Ştefan Harko 103.50;
    86th Place: Iosif Focht 100.55

Prague, 1962

Team, Women

    9th Place: Romania 366.920.

Individual All-Around, Women

    20th Place: Sonia Iovan 75.363;
    44th Place: Emilia Liţă 73.530;
    50th Place: Atanasia Ionescu 73.231;
    55th Place: Elena Dobrovolschi 72.897;
    72nd Place: Mariana Ilie 71.499;
    116th Place: Ana Mărgineanu 17.099 (injured).

Individual All-Around, Men

    71st Place: Frederic Orendi 108.80;
    95th Place: Gheorghe Tobăneanu 106.55.

Dortmund, 1966

Individual All-Around, Women

    28th Place: Elena Ceampelea 74.132;
    58th Place: Elena Tutan 71.863.

Lublijana, 1970

Team, Women

    5th Place: Romania 364.50.

Individual All-Around, Women

    17th Place: Elena Ceampelea 74.30;
    24th Place: Paula Ioan 72.95;
    30th Place: Elisabeta Turcu 72.45;
    31st Place: Alina Goreac 72.20;
    36th Place: Olga Ştefan 71.70;
    41st Place: Rodica Apăteanu 71.25.

Team, Men

8th Place: Romania 536.55.

Individual All-Around, Men

28th Place: Petre Mihaiuc 108.45;
35th Place: Mircea Gheorghiu 107.45;
41st Place: Gheorghe Păunescu 106.65;
42nd Place: Nicolae Achim 106.35;
52nd Place: Dan Grecu 105.55;
66th Place: Gheorghe Tobăneanu 104.30.

Varna, 1974

Team, Women

4th Place: Romania 369.30.

Individual All-Around, Women

8th Place: Alina Goreac 75.925;
12th Place: Anca Grigoraş 75.125;
16th Place: Aurelia Dobre 74.150;
29th Place: Elena Ceampelea 73.325;
32nd Place: Rodica Sabău 72.475;
34th Place: Paula Ioan 71.650.

Apparatus Finals, Women

Vault, 4th Place: Alina Goreac 19.025;
Balance Beam, 5th Place: Alina Goreac 18.905.

Team, Men

6th Place: Romania (16. Dan Grecu 111.60; 29. Nicolae Oprescu 109.45; 43. Gheorghe Păunescu 107.75; 44. Mihai Borş 107.55; 49. Constantin Petrescu 107.30; 52. Ştefan Gal 107.20) 547.25.

Individual All-Around, Men

18th Place: Dan Grecu 111.200;
35th Place: Nicolae Oprescu 100.875.

Apparatus Finals, Men

Rings, 1st Place: Dan Grecu 19.525.

Strasbourg, 1978

Team, Women

2nd Place: Romania (Nadia Comăneci, Emilia Eberle, Teodora Ungureanu, Marilena Vlădăran, Marilena Neacşu, Anca Grigoraş) 384.25.

Individual All-Around, Women

4th Place: Nadia Comăneci 77.725;
5th Place: Emilia Eberle 77.300;
15th Place: Marilena Neacşu 76.275.

Apparatus Finals, Women

Vault, 2nd Place: Nadia Comăneci 19.600; 5th Place: Emilia Eberle 19.450;
Parallel Bars, 3rd Place: Emilia Eberle 19.625: 5th Place: Nadia Comăneci 19.575;
Balance Beam, 1st Place: Nadia Comăneci 19.625; 3rd Place: Emilia Eberle 19.575;
Floor Exercise, 3rd Place: Emilia Eberle 19.525; 8th Place: Nadia Comăneci 19.250.

Team, Men

7th Place: Romania (Dan Grecu, Kurt Szilier, Ion Checicheş, Aurelian Georgescu, Sorin Cepoi, Nicolae Oprescu) 560.85.

Individual All-Around, Men

23rd Place: Kurt Szilier 112.975;
24th Place: Dan Grecu 112.900;
25th Place: Ion Checicheş 112.775.

Apparatus Finals, Men

Rings, 3rd Place: Dan Grecu 19.650; 7th Place: Nicolae Oprescu 19.325.

Fort Worth, 1979

Team, Women

1st Place: Romania (Nadia Comăneci, Emilia Eberle, Dumitriţa Turner, Melita Ruhn, Rodica Dunca, Marilena Vlădărău) 389.550.

Individual all-Around, Women

4th Place: Melita Ruhn 78.250;
7th Place: Emilia Eberle 77.350;
8th Place: Rodica Dunca 77.350.

Apparatus Finals, Women

Vault, 1st Place: Dumitriţa Turner 19.775; 7th Place: Melita Ruhn 19.475;
Parallel Bars, 3rd Place: Emilia Eberle 19.750;
Balance Beam, 8th Place: Melita Ruhn 18.975;
Floor Exercise, 1st Place: Emilia Eberle 19.800; 3rd Place: Melita Ruhn 19.725.

Team, Men

8th Place: Romania (Dan Grecu, Kurt Szilier, Sorin Cepoi, Ion Checicheş, Aurelian Georgescu, Nicolae Oprescu) 569.750.

Individual All-Around, Men

23rd Place: Dan Grecu 114.650;
26th Place: Kurt Szilier 114.275;
30th Place: Aurelian Georgescu 113.650.

Apparatus Finals, Men

Rings, 2nd Place: Dan Grecu 19.700.

Moscova, 1981

Team, Women

4th Place: Romania (Mihaela Stănuleţ, Dumitriţa Turner, Rodica Dunca, Emilia Eberle, Lavinia Agache, Cristina Grigoraş) 381.50.

Individual All-Around, Women

5th Place: Cristina Grigoraş 77.125;
6th Place: Rodica Dunca 77.025;
7th Place: Lavinia Agache 76.900.

Apparatus Finals, Women

Vault, 5th Place: Lavinia Agache 19.275;
Parallel Bars, 5th Place: Cristina Grigoraş 19.650;
7th Place: Lavinia Agache 19.450;
Balance Beam, 8th Place: Rodica Dunca 18.625;
Floor Exercise, 5th Place: Rodica Dunca 19.450.

Team, Men

9th Place: Romania (Octavian Ionaşiu, Valentin Pantea, Dumitru Sârbu, Aurelian Georgescu, Emilian Nicula, Kurt Szilier) 570.60.

Individual All-Around, Men

24th Place: Emilian Nicula 115.275;
28th Place: Kurt Szilier 114.775;
30th Place: Aurelian Georgescu 114.325.

Budapest, 1983

Team, Women

2nd Place: Romania (Simona Renciu, Mirela Barbălată, Laura Cutina, Mihaela Stănuleţ, Ecaterina Szabo, Lavinia Agache) 392.10.

Individual All-Around, Women

3rd Place: Ecaterina Szabo 78.975;
6th Place: Lavinia Agache 78.575;
9th Place: Laura Cutina 78.275.

Apparatus Finals, Women

Vault, 2nd Place: Lavinia Agache 19.800; 2nd Place: Ecaterina Szabo 19.800;
Parallel Bars, 2nd Place: Lavinia Agache 19.800; 2nd Place: Ecaterina Szabo 19.800;
Balance Beam, 3rd Place: Lavinia Agache 19.675;
Floor Exercise, 1st Place: Ecaterina Szabo 19.975; 4th Place: Lavinia Agache 19.800.

Team, Men

11th Place: Romania (Octavian Ionaşiu, Aurelian Georgescu, Dan Odorhean, Molnar Levente, Valentin Pântea, Emilian Nicula) 573.70.

Individual All-Around, Men

20th Place; Emilian Nicula 115.975.

Apparatus Finals, Men

Rings, 7th Place: Molnar Levente 19.700.

Montreal, 1985

Team, Women

2nd Place: Romania (Ecaterina Szabo, Daniela Silivaş, Camelia Voinea, Laura Cutina, Eugenia Golea, Celestina Popa) 388.850.

Individual All-Around, Women

5th Place: Ecaterina Szabo 78.088;
7th place: Daniela Silivaş 77.825;
9th Place: Camelia Voinea 77.050.

Apparatus Finals, Women

Vault, 2nd Place: Ecaterina Szabo 19.650;
Parallel Bars, 4th Place: Camelia Voinea 19.463;
6th Place: Ecaterina Szabo 19.413;
Balance Beam, 1st Place: Daniela Silivaş 19.813; 2nd Place: Ecaterina Szabo 19.775;
Floor Exercise, 4th Place: Daniela Silivaş 19.713; 4th Place: Ecaterina Szabo 19.713.

Individual All-Around, Men

32nd Place: Emilian Nicula 112.525; Valentin Pântea 110.700.

Rotterdam, 1987

Team, Women

1st Place: Romania (Aurelia Dobre, Daniela Silivaş, Ecaterina Szabo, Camelia Voinea, Eugenia Golea, Celestina Popa) 395.400.

Individual All-Around, Women

1st Place: Aurelia Dobre 79.650;
3rd Place: Daniela Silivaş 79.200;
14th Place: Ecaterina Szabo 77.375.

Aurelia Dobre

Apparatus Finals, Women

Vault, 2nd Place: Eugenia Golea 19.857; 3rd Place: Aurelia Dobre, 19.844;
Parallel Bars, 1st Place: Daniela Silivaş 19.925; 4th Place: Aurelia Dobre 19.862;
Balance Beam, 1st Place: Aurelia Dobre 19.950; 3rd Place: Ecaterina Szabo 19.737;
Floor Exercise, 1st Place: Daniela Silivaş 20.000; 3rd Place: Aurelia Dobre 19.950.

Team, Men

7th Place: Romania (Marius Gherman, Valentin Pântea, Marius Tobă, Emilian Nicula, Marian Rizan, Adrian Sandu) 573.300.

Individual All-Around, Men

19th Place: Marius Gherman 115.825;
24th Place: Marius Tobă 115.425;
31st Place: Valentin Pântea 114.950.

Apparatus Finals, Men

Parallel Bars, 6th Place: Marian Rizan 19.575.

Stuttgart, 1989

Team, Women

2nd Place: Romania (Daniela Silivaş, Gabriela Potorac, Cristina Bontaş, Eugenia Popa, Aurelia Dobre, Lăcrămioara Filip) 394.931.

Individual All-Around, Women

4th Place: Cristina Bontaş 39.762;
12th Place: Daniela Silivaş 39.312;
16th Place: Gabriela Potorac 39.074.

Apparatus Finals, Women

Vault, 2nd Place: Cristina Bontaş 9.950; 6th Place: Gabriela Potorac 9.743;
Parallel Bars, 1st Place: Daniela Silivaş 10.000; 5th Place: Gabriela Potorac 9.925;
Balance Beam, 1st Place: Daniela Silivaş 9.950; 3rd Place: Gabriela Potorac 9.887;
Floor Exercise, 1st Place: Daniela Silivaş 10.000; 3rd Place: Cristina Bontaş 9.962

Team, Men

6th Place: Romania (Marius Gherman, Marian Stoican, Marian Rizan) 572.450.

Individual All-Around, Men

8th Place: Marius Gherman 58.450;
21st Place: Marian Stoican 57.350;
24th Place: Marian Rizan 56.950.

Apparatus Finals, Men

Floor Exercise, 4th Place: Marius Gherman;
Pommel Horse, 4th Place: Marian Rizan;
Vault, 4th Place: Marius Gherman; 6th Place: Marian Stoican;
Parallel Bars, 5th Place: Marian Rizan.

Indianapolis, 1991

Team, Women

3rd Place: Romania (Cristina Bontaş, Lavinia Miloşovici, Vanda Hădărean, Mirela Paşca, Maria Neculiţă, Eugenia Popa) 393.841.

Individual All-Around, Women

3rd Place: Cristina Bontaş 39.711;
7th Place: Lavinia Miloşovici 39.474;
8th Place: Mirela Paşca 39.336.

Apparatus Finals, Women

Vault, 1st Place: Lavinia Miloşovici 9.949; 4th Place: Cristina Bontaş 9.881;
Parallel Bars, 4th Place: Mirela Paşca 9.937; 7th Place: Cristina Bontaş 9.862;
Balance Beam, 3rd Place: Lavinia Miloşovici 9.900; 8th Place: Cristina Bontaş 9.412;
Floor Exercise, 1st Place: Cristina Bontaş 9.962; 4th Place: Lavinia Miloşovici 9.925.

Team, Men

9th Place: Romania (Nicolae Bejenaru, Adrian Cătănoiu, Marian Rizan, Adrian Sandu, Adrian Gal, Marius Gherman) 565.425.

Individual All-Around, Men

23rd Place: Marius Gherman 57.200;
28th Place: Adrian Gal 56.950;
31st Place: Adrian Cătănoiu 56.800.

Paris, 1992

Apparatus Finals, Women

Vault, 4th Place: Lavinia Miloşovici 9.906; 7th Place: Gina Gogean 9.600;
Parallel Bars, 1st Place: Lavinia Miloşovici 9.950; 3rd Place: Mirela Paşca 9.887;
Balance Beam, 2nd Place: Maria Neculiţă 9.850; 9th Place: Gina Gogean 8.750;
Floor Exercise, 3rd Place: Maria Neculiţă 9.887; 8th Place: Lavinia Miloşovici 9.300.

Apparatus Finals, Men

Floor Exercise, 4th Place: Marius Gherman 9.600;
Vault, 5th Place: Marius Gherman 9.543.

Birmingham, 1993

Individual All-Around, Women

2nd Place: Gina Gogean 39.055;
8th Place: Lavinia Miloşovici 38.392.

Apparatus Finals, Women

Vault, 2nd Place: Lavinia Miloşovici 9.737; 4th Place: Gina Gogean;
Parallel Bars, 3rd Place: Andreea Cacovean 9.787; 5th Place: Lavinia Miloşovici 9.500;
Balance Beam, 1st Place: Lavinia Miloşovici 9.850; 3rd Place: Gina Gogean 9.650;
Floor Exercise, 2nd Place: Gina Gogean 9.737; 5th Place: Lavinia Miloşovici 9.675.

Individual All-Around, Men

15th Place: Marius Gherman 54.100;
19th Place: Alexandru Ciucă 53.575.

Apparatus Finals, Men

Floor Exercise, 5th Place: Marius Gherman 9.150;
Pommel Horse, 7th Place: Alexandru Ciucă 8.575;
Rings, 5th Place: Dan Burincă 9.412;
High Bar, 2nd Place: Marius Gherman 9.375.

Brisbane, 1994

Individual All-Around, Women

2nd Place: Lavinia Miloşovici 39.236;
4th Place: Gina Gogean 39.061;
8th Place: Nadia Hăţăgan 38.836.

Apparatus Finals, Women

Vault, 1st Place: Gina Gogean 9.812; 3rd Place: Lavinia Miloşovici 9.787;
Parallel Bars, 6th Place: Lavinia Miloşovici 9.250; 7th Place: Nadia Hăţăgan 9.137;
Balance Beam: 4th Place: Nadia Hăţăgan 9.687; 5th Place: Lavinia Miloşovici 9.675;
Floor Exercise, 2nd Place: Lavinia Miloşovici 9.837; 3rd Place: Gina Gogean 9.687.

Individual All-Around, Men

18th Place: Nicu Stroia 55.062;
37th Place: Marius Urzică 53.300;
44th Place: Marius Gherman 52.950.

Apparatus Finals, Men

> Pommel Horse, 1st Place: Marius Urzică 9.712;
> Rings, 3rd Place: Dan Burincă 9.700.

Dortmund, 1994

Team, Women

> 1st Place: Romania (Lavinia Miloşovici, Gina Gogean, Nadia Hăţăgan, Daniela Mărănducă, Ionela Loaieş, Simona Amânar, Claudia Presăcan) 195.847.

Team, Men

> 10th Place: Romania (Marius Gherman, Dan Burincă, Adrian Ianculescu, Cristian Leric, Nistor Şandro, Robert Tăciuleţ, Adrian Sandu) 269.650.

Sabae, 1995

Team, Women

> 1st Place: Romania (Lavinia Miloşovici, Gina Gogean, Simona Amânar, Alexandra Marinescu, Claudia Presăcan, Andreea Cacovean) 387.865.

Individual All-Around, Women

> 3rd Place: Lavinia Miloşovici 39,086;
> 4th Place: Simona Amânar 39.049;
> 14th Place: Gina Gogean 38.250.

Apparatus Finals, Women

> Vault, 1st Place: Simona Amânar 9.781; 3rd Place: Gina Gogean 9.706;
> Parallel Bars, 4th Place: Alexandra Marinescu 9.800; 5th Place: Lavinia Miloşovici 9.775;

> Balance Beam, 4th place: Alexandra Marinescu 9.737;
> Floor Exercise, 1st Place: Gina Gogean 9.825; 6th Place: Simona Amânar 9.437.

Team, Men

> 3rd Place: Romania (Cristian Leric, Nistor Şandro, Marius Urzică, Adrian Ianculescu, Nicolae Bejenaru, Nicu Stroia, Dan Burincă) 561.947.

Individual All-Around, Men

> 11th Place: Cristian Leric 56.536;
> 34th Place: Nistor Şandro 53.975;
> 36th Place: Adrian Ianculescu 50.900.

Apparatus Finals, Men

> Pommel Horse, 4th Place: Marius Urzică 9.725;
> Rings, 2nd Place: Dan Burincă 9.762;
> Vault, 5th Place: Cristian Leric 9.606; 8th Place: Adrian Ianculescu 9.312;
> High Bar, 6th Place: Nistor Şandro 9.687.

San Juan, 1996

Apparatus Finals, Women

> Vault, 1st Place: Gina Gogean 9.800; 2nd Place: Simona Amânar 9.787;
> Parallel Bars, 11th Place: Lavinia Miloşovici 9.637;
> Balance Beam, 2nd Place: Alexandra Marinescu 9.812; 8th Place: Gina Gogean 9. 075;
> Floor Exercise, 1st Place: Gina Gogean 9.850; 3rd Place: Lavinia Miloşovici 9.800.

Apparatus Finals, Men

> Rings, 4th Place: Dan Burincă 9.712.

HISTRIA
BOOKS

VITA HISTRIA

GAUDIUM

Addison & Highsmith

CENTER FOR Romanian STUDIES

EXCELLENCE IN PUBLISHING SINCE 1996

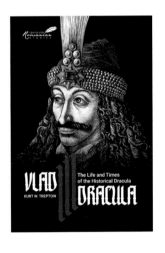

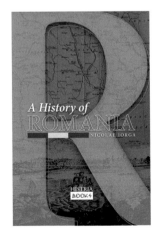
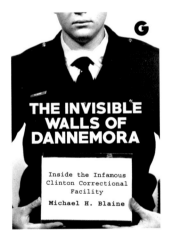

AVAILABLE AT

HISTRIABOOKS.COM